Alfred's Basic Piano Library
# Piano
## Classic Themes
### Level 5

### Allan Small

This book contains new arrangements of great *Classic Themes*. Many of these beautiful melodies were not originally written for the keyboard. Composers write music in many instrumental forms—symphonies, concertos, ballets, etc. Allan Small has taken some of the most popular and arranged them in graded order for the piano student. Also included are arrangements of vocal music. There is music from popular operas as well as folk music, music that was passed down from one generation to another and whose composers are frequently unknown.

The purpose of this series of *Classic Themes* is to allow the piano student to become familiar with these beautiful melodies by performing them. Though not in any way a substitute for the original composition, *Classic Themes*, through its arrangements and

write-ups for each selection, will give the student a heightened awareness of many composers and their works. By performing these arrangements and by listening to the recordings of the compositions in their original form, the student will gain an expanded understanding of and appreciation for the truly great music of the past.

The four books of *Classic Themes*, Levels 2–5, are designed to supplement ALFRED'S BASIC PIANO LIBRARY and are coordinated page-by-page with the LESSON BOOKS. The instructions in the upper right corner of the first page of each piece clearly indicate when the student is ready to learn the piece. The pieces may be played at any time after the designated pages are covered, but it is best not to attempt them sooner than these references indicate.

Angel's Serenade (Braga)................................................22
Annen Polka (Strauss).................................................20
Aria from "Don Giovanni" (Mozart)...............................28
Drinking Song from "La Traviata" (Verdi).........................8
Estudiantina (Waldteufel)............................................16
Forsaken (Koschat)....................................................19
Gypsy Dance from "Carmen" (Bizet)................................2
June Barcarolle (Tchaikovsky) ......................................4
Last Rose of Summer, The (Moore)................................30
Lesson 2 (Hook)..........................................................6
Love's Greeting (Elgar)...............................................29
Mirror Dance from "Faust" (Gounod) .............................24
Piano Concerto No. 2, Opening Themes (Rachmaninoff) ....10
Piano Concerto No. 21, Theme from (Mozart)...................12
Prelude, Op. 28, No. 20 (Chopin) ..................................32
Tambourin (Rameau) ..................................................14
To a Wild Rose (MacDowell).........................................26
Toreador Song from "Carmen" (Bizet)............................18

*Use after BRAZILIAN HOLIDAY,
LESSON BOOK 5 (page 2).*

Georges Bizet (1838–1875) was a distinguished French composer whose opera *Carmen* shocked the audiences of Europe when it premiered. The main character is Carmen, a Gypsy woman of strong character. Bizet is said to have used many original Gypsy tunes and popular Spanish songs for sources in the opera.

# Gypsy Dance
## from "Carmen"

Georges Bizet

4

*Use after SWAN LAKE (page 4).*

This is one of a set of pieces Tchaikovsky composed (one for each month of the year).  A barcarolle is a song of the Venetian gondoliers.  The left-hand patterns should bring to mind the lapping of the waves as they break against the boat.

# June Barcarolle

Peter Ilyich Tchaikovsky

# Lesson 2

*Use after BAGATELLE (page 8).*

James Hook (1746–1827) was an organist and composer. *Lesson 2* is a piece for piano written for his students in the style of a dance.

James Hook

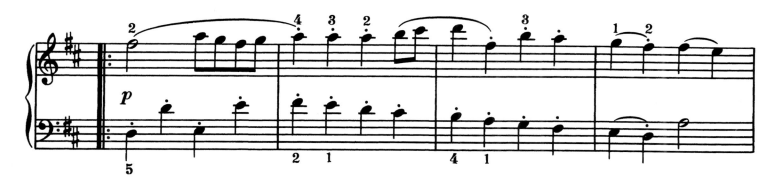

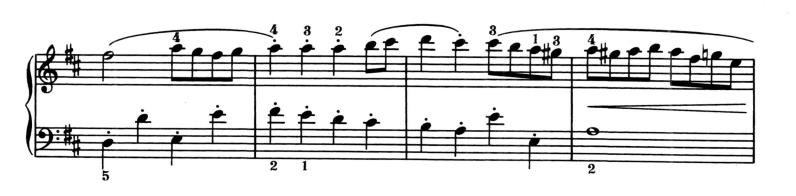

*Use after BAGATELLE (page 8).*

Verdi's opera *La Traviata* (The Wayward Woman) premiered at a time when revolutionary forces were trying to unite the many small states of Italy into a single government. Verdi, by writing such rousing peasantlike tunes as the *Drinking Song*, did his small part in encouraging the people to band together for Italy's unification.

# Drinking Song
## from "La Traviata"

Giuseppe Verdi

*Use after SONATINA (page 13).*

This piano concerto appeared as a light at the end of a tunnel of great depression for Rachmaninoff; he had been deeply disturbed by the lack of success of his early works. His family sent him to an extraordinary psychiatrist, and after a year of treatment, Rachmaninoff produced the *Piano Concerto No. 2* and dedicated it to the helpful doctor. It remains as one of the most beloved concertos of all time.

## Opening Themes from
# Piano Concerto No. 2

Sergei Rachmaninoff

**Moderato e espressivo**

D. C. al ⊕, then Coda

poco ritardando

⊕ Coda

ritardando

*Use after THEME (page 15).*

This theme from the slow movement of Mozart's *Piano Concerto No. 21* was used as background music for a popular film several years ago entitled *Elvira Madigan*.

# Theme from
# Piano Concerto No. 21

Wolfgang Amadeus Mozart

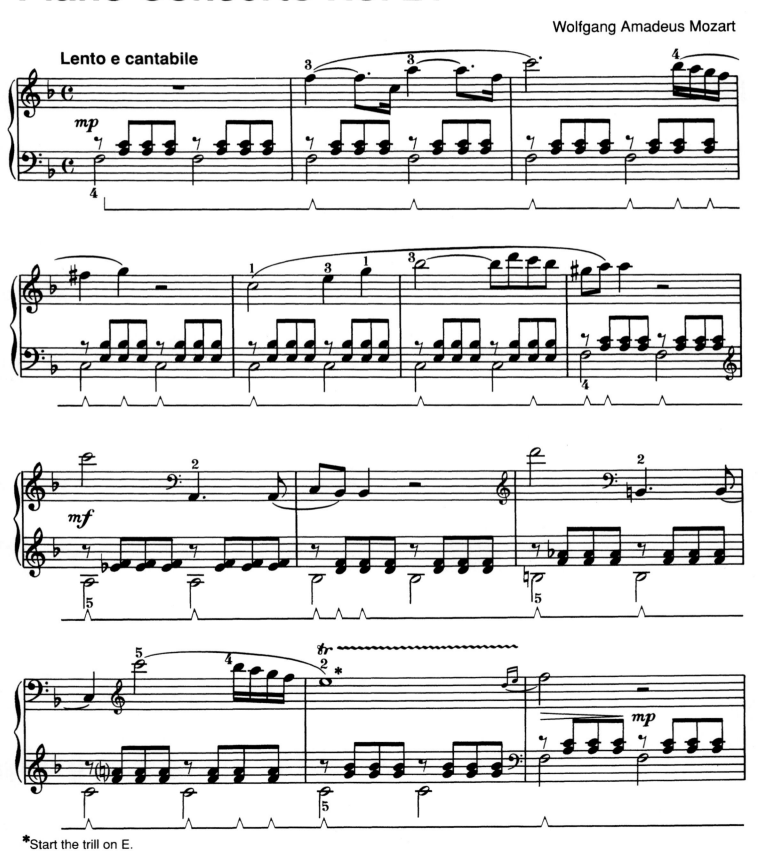

*Start the trill on E.

13

*Use after THE TAILOR'S SONG (page 20).*

Jean-Philippe Rameau (1683–1764) was an eminent composer and writer on music theory. He played the harpsichord at 7 years of age and could read at sight any piece of music. The tambourin is a drum, imitated in the left-hand part of this lively dance.

# Tambourin

Jean-Philippe Rameau

*D. C. al Fine*

*Use after SPANISH DANCE (page 22).*

Émile Waldteufel (1837–1915) composed many waltzes, including the ever-popular *Skater's Waltz*. Waldteufel uses many devices for contrast in *Estudiantina*; the A sections are in minor, soft, and with short motives, while the B section moves to the relative major, is loud, and persists with spiraling scale passages.

# Estudiantina
## (Major and Minor Themes)

**Allegretto**

(B minor)

Émile Waldteufel

**D. C. al 𝄌, then Coda**

𝄌 *Coda*

*Use after A VERY SPECIAL DAY (page 26).*

The majesty of the bullfighter's march to the ring is portrayed in this magnificent excerpt from Bizet's opera, *Carmen*. When deciding on the tempo, remember the bullfighters may not be too anxious to get to the ring, so take your time!

# Toreador Song
## from "Carmen"

Georges Bizet

*A sixteenth-note triplet equals the time value of 1 eighth note or 2 sixteenth notes.

*Use after A VERY SPECIAL DAY (page 26).*

The melody of this tender piece is beautifully placed into the alto voice of the texture (lower notes in the treble clef), until it emerges on top at measure 13. The upper voice of the bass clef, in syncopated rhythm, should be kept very soft to let the alto sing through.

# Forsaken

Thomas Koschat

*Use after A VERY SPECIAL DAY (page 26).*

Dedicated to Queen Anne of Austria by the waltz king, Johann Strauss Jr., this polka
should be played at a rather slow tempo as indicated by the metronome marking.
Remember to sustain the half-notes in the left hand.

# Annen Polka

Johann Strauss, Jr.

**Rather delicately** (♪ = 116, 120)

*Use after MAGIC CARPET RIDE  (page 29).*

The *Angel's Serenade,* with it's beautiful melody, is a song about a child who, cradled in its mother's arms, describes the song of angels.  It was extremely popular in the 30s when the Victor recording, sung by Irish tenor John McCormack and accompanied by the legendary violinist Fritz Kreisler, sold over one million copies.  It was composed by Gaetano Braga  (1829–1907).

# Angel's Serenade

**Moderato con moto**

Gaetano Braga

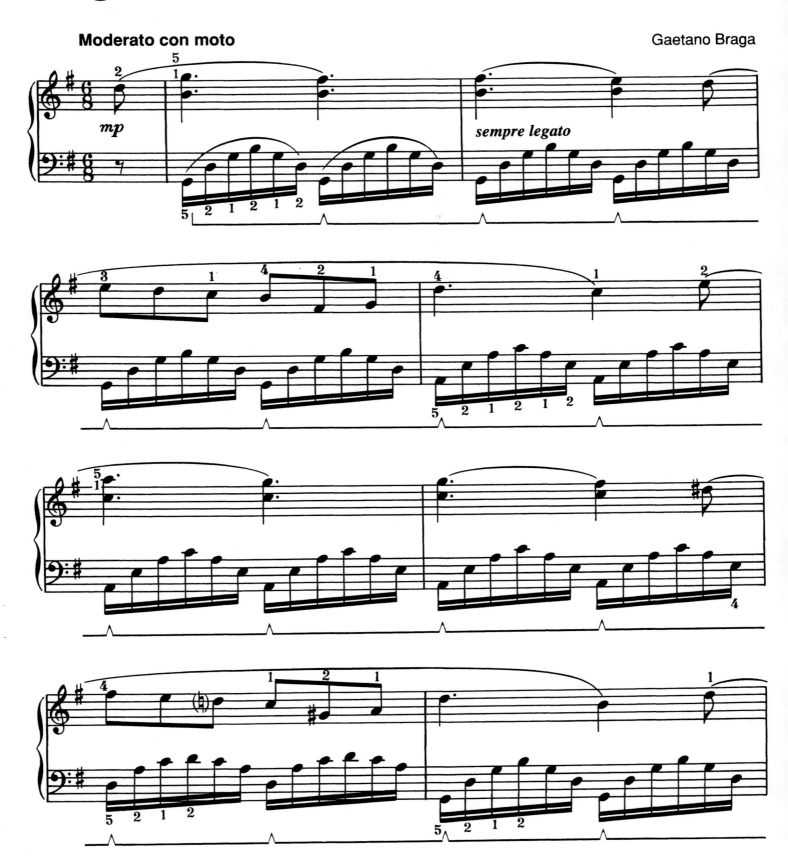

*Use after MAGIC CARPET RIDE (page 29).*

Charles Gounod (1818–1893) was descended from a family of artists; his father was a painter. Gounod was a thorough musician and master of the orchestra. His most popular opera is *Faust*.

# Mirror Dance
## from "Faust"

Charles Gounod

**Allegretto grazioso**

*Use after MINIATURE OVERTURE (page 32).*

Edward MacDowell (1860–1908) was an American composer who wrote many compositions for orchestra, voice, piano, etc. On his death his widow donated his summer home to be utilized as a residence for artists working in music and art. The piece is from a set titled *Woodland Sketches*.

# To a Wild Rose

Edward MacDowell

*Use after SONATA (page 34).*

Mozart called his *Don Giovanni* a dramma giocoso rather than an opera; a dramma giocoso is a comic opera that has some serious characters as well. The serious characters are usually from the aristocratic class, while the comic characters are often servants and peasants. This aria is generally serious and elegant in character, but snatches of humor appear at the cadence points in measures 8, 12 and 22.

# Aria
## from "Don Giovanni"

Wolfgang Amadeus Mozart

**Moderato grazioso con moto**

*Use after THE MARRIAGE OF FIGARO (page 38).*

Sir Edward Elgar (British) grew up in musical surroundings.  He was a prolific composer with more than 85 compositions in various categories to his credit.  Since it was written, his *Pomp and Circumstance* march has been played at nearly every school graduation ceremony.

# Love's Greeting
## (Salut d'Amour)

Edward Elgar

30

*Use after THE MARRIAGE OF FIGARO (page 38).*

Thomas Moore (1779–1852) was both poet and musician. During his lifetime his many songs were very popular. *The Last Rose of Summer* is still sung by many vocalists.

# The Last Rose of Summer

Thomas Moore

*Use after PRELUDE IN C MINOR (page 42).*

Chopin manages to convey a deep sense of sorrow in a short composition of only thirteen measures. It is also a lesson in beautiful harmony. Note the descending bass in the fifth and sixth measures. The famous conductor Arturo Toscanini once said, "If you want to understand harmony, study Chopin."

# Prelude
## Op. 28, No. 20

Frédéric Chopin